Heart Map
and the Song of Our Ancestors

מפת הלב

ושיר אבותינו

Poems by Devon Spier

Illustrations by Kandace Boos

Printed in the United States of America

First Printing, 2018

ISBN [placeholder 1-77538020-3]

Author: Devon Spier
Illustrator: Kandace Boos
Editor: Hila Ratzabi
Layout and Design: Kevin Romoser

CONTENTS

Forgetfulness leads to exile.
In remembrance lies the secret to redemption.

Ba'al Shem Tov

TO THE READER

You are not now nor are you ever alone.
Your ancestors are walking with you.
Every step of the way.

Jews are the people of the continual going forth. We are
constantly surviving in ways that transform the heart of the
world and each other, too.

Yet, with this movement comes a paradox: For after all those
years of bondage, each of us is still there, bound to a past that
is constantly replaying itself in the broken parts of our lives.

Our communities are adept at talking our pain. We know the
stories of the six million, the besieged walls, and the Pharaohs
that rose up against us in every generation. Our triumph and
our grief is the story stuff of seder tables whose tellings will
wind on through the millennia.

But the fleeing and the witnessing hold onto us as memories
that cannot be erased. And the pain paralyzes us in continuous
moving. For how many of us suffer reenactments of our
people's pasts, fueled by the relentless pursuit of something we
don't fully understand?

This constant going forth has been the foundation of our
People's uniqueness, our religious and cultural output, and

our world-given gift. And it has also fostered a bereaved automatism, pushing us to keep going when all that life back there and ahead tugs at us to stop for a moment, open up the past, and feel.

It's a fearful proposition. To have survived all that life back there only to be wounded somehow here. But trauma, let alone Jewish trauma, is not a weakness. Nor is it damaging or damning.

After all, in the words of the Ba'al Shem Tov:

"Forgetfulness leads to exile. In remembrance lies the secret to redemption."

This truth is what led me to begin writing ancestor poetry. I was 29 and in the midst of the hardest year of my life. The shtetl dweller in me wanted to keep going, and the spirit G-d put within me said stop for a while, be with our tradition's words, and heal.

For memory can be a life-giving choosing, if we let it be. And when we choose to voice the unspoken parts of our paths and walk with our tradition in a way that enhances what we hold deep within ourselves, the seeds of transformation and release take root.

And it is in affirmation of the Tree of Life that I invite you in to enjoin yourself with the paths of your ancestors. To pour yourself into these pages. And to bring to light what has long been buried deep.

Not out of obligation or fear. Or because you or your past are in need of fixing or moralizing. But because no matter what you are facing, your Jewish past is available for the seeding. By walking the past home in the present, we have the power, at long last, to become masters of our lives and our fates. And at long last, להיות עם חופשי, "to be a People that is truly free."

1.

ABRAHAM IN THE IDOL SHOP

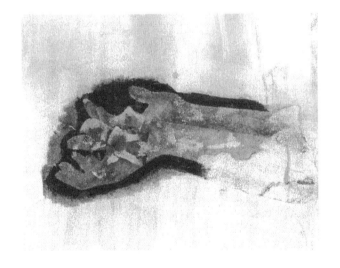

Come close and listen before speaking.
Put aside the Psalms,
The King's sagely ring.
And flip open the first page
In your great book.
There, pour out the ink of your soul
And let the drops fall off the page,
Never passing a moment to witness.
The falling and the absence of color.
Follow the trail
Of every last drop
Then behold the door to the room
That is really a heart.

The place for which we have been searching is always the place
in which we have secretly been standing.

These are the generations.
And we, too, are the generations.
Our speaking is tied to their speaking.
And our living is tied to their living.

We are not merely connected like two ends of a thread.
We are the thread.
One and whole.

But any unraveling
Or tearing
Pulls apart us all.

It was as if angels' prayers poured out of my mouth
And ancestral wrestling sang out of my limbs.

And I knew no matter how I was made
I could be remade
In the holy unmaking of this sacred moment.

Miriam by the riverbank
Prophesizing our deliverance
Looking ever forward
Yet cast out by false sight
Not hers but his.
A father who could not behold the reach of her senses.
But still, she knew, we would eventually be redeemed.

And despite the gulf
She moved
Chanted
Danced.

And neither accusation nor illness
Could dry the wise, old well of our girl's seeing soul.

Perhaps I, too, am pregnant.
And my womb? The world.
Containing not the fruits of future generations
But two opposite poles
Pulling at me.
Pleading with me.
"For our sake, give away your soul."

"If so, why do I exist?," you surmise.
For to give life, I, like you, must perish a little.
And to carry others, I, like you, am expected to empty myself
    in full.

I have been cast out and disparaged.
My soul ever-living amid the darkness of the dead.

For who is holy, among those who dismiss the young?
And readily discard the old?

Am I to stand here, roots withering, with the world's
	ruthlessness upon me?
For woe has become me.
And compassion has left me, visiting itself upon more sinful
	folk than I.

But, Your word, Creator.
Letters larger than life.
More overflowing than this most bitter cup.

Pain and joy are fleeting.
But your Truth is eternity,
Enduring.

Away from the palace and the bulrushes,
All the riches and the striking,
Is the place where my path of un-becoming,
Of diverting,
Has been revealed.

My whole life I have been a prince enslaved.
Not to Pharoah.
But to the illusion that I am
Who I am not.
How I will greet you, Ceaseless Becomer,
I cannot say.
But as I remove what you have asked of me
I pray for the strength to witness my true self.

That I will be who I am meant to be.
And become.

How do we decide to be who we are meant to be?
Are we to unfurl a scroll and walk the length of our ancestors?
Are we to go forth, like Abraham to Canaan?
Or stay behind, like Moses who arrived just shy of the
    Promised Land?
No matter our steps
No matter how measured or unsure
Let the desert and its mystery
Wrap us in a Greater Knowing
That our selves, like our ancestors, are bound up in the
    journey
And that with every twist and turn,
G-d, and we, too
Resiliently and revealingly
Remain.

Our tribe contains tribes.
Tribes forged by circumstance and cemented by our own
    choosing.

Prophets who once bowed before idols.
And artists who rebuked even prophets.

Monarchs who kept guard over a land.
And a People made humble by the wilderness.

However you belong.
However you came to be.
Know that you, too, are numerous as the stars of heaven.

And that whether you are hard as rock, soft as psalms
Or even as mysterious as a basket in the bulrushes

Your arc reveals our covenant.

My questions lead me in and beyond myself.
Like roots in the ground, they pull me down to what was
And like buds on a tree, they remind me of what's in front of me
In bloom and changing
And grounded as an old tree trunk.
Will my questions outlive my past?
Will my present thrive with my questions?
One can never tell
But one can always ask.
Praise to the G-d who knows and who doesn't
And the People who flourish in wonder.

I am not off the *derekh*.
But I am off the grid.
Here there are no cups for anointing
Or even a burning bush for the seeing.
But a great opening like the river of psalms.
Words smashing against the rocks of tradition
And images arising as a current that carries my soul steadily
    downstream.
Where? I can't begin to say.
But of all the paths that were chosen for me
I take refuge in the one that moves freely.
Flowing into the sea of life by the gift of my own choosing.

When the outside is remote and uncertain
And the inside is steady and bleak
We can subsume ourselves in the tethering
Or look closer until we see the unseen.
We can study our contours.
Cast light upon shadows.
Make known all the silent holdings.
Release the yoke of this rope.
And with our soul's sight
We can walk through the illusion of theological geometry
And climb into the ever-present infinity:
There is no fortress or breach
Only boundless, available space.

The tale of Rabbi Adam Ba'al Shem of Ropczyce
Is likewise a tale of the shtetl-dweller who found himself
    standing at his door.
The *yid* knocked and then entered,
Finding himself, in a short while, the initiate of a secret society
    that fixed all the *pashut yidden* (simple Jews) of Europe.
That turned their souls heaven-ward to G-d.
But, alas, the unwritten story.
Of the moment between knock and entry:
For, the *yid*'s generations
Stood all in the same place.
Knocking at their hearts.
And crying:
"What of the *yidden* who do not need fixing?
Who crave the safety of arms opened?
Of lives unencumbered by a master's tutelage or ever-watchful gaze?"
O, G-d!
O, Maker!
Of this old and living soul!
Assure me that the path before me
Began so long ago.
That my wandering is not only ancient
But holy tradition.
And no matter master's house
or shtetl abode,
Wherever I stand, I am in the shelter of the ancestors.

בָּרוּךְ אַתָּה יְיָ הַפּוֹרֵשׂ סֻכַּת שָׁלוֹם עָלֵינוּ וְעַל כָּל
עַמּוֹ יִשְׂרָאֵל וְעַל יְרוּשָׁלָיִם

Blessed are You, Eternal G-d, whose shelter of peace is spread over us, over all Your People, and over Jerusalem. Amen.

*Original story based on narratives shared by Martin Buber & Gershom Scholem

Blessed are the stars
Not the ones we can see from Earth
Or even the ones in Olam Haba
But the ones who shimmer in the unseen places
Who reside in student ghettos
Hospital waiting rooms and bus stations
Who linger behind front desks and in back rooms
And speak words like "sweetheart"
And "I can help you fill that out, dear"
The ones who make our coffees
Who remember our names, even when we met once
Years passed
Who look beyond family or familiarity
And with the expanse of the galaxy
Dare to embrace us, too.

I took an oath.
For land and long life.
Though when?
I cannot remember.
But there was fire.
And I was spared.

Years passed.
My looking forward ceased.
And as I looked down,
I found.
There was blood on my hands.

I clocked more miles.
But now, I am trading in walking.
For the moment to stand and face my sin.

Will my pain dissuade me?
Will my past betray me?

I have no answer.
Just that long and final walk between surrender and siege.

And angels.
I could have sworn I heard the voices of angels.
Crying, "Spare him."

But I wasn't sure if they meant him.
Or me.

There is something sacred
When we find ourselves upside down.
Only there do we discover that each of our movements is part
    of a larger circle
Whose center leads us to our own inner knowing.
And yes, too, the ultimate meaning of
"Turn it and turn it again."
Which does not merely apply to the Law
But to every last life on earth.

For those who choose human beings, try
        choosing Torah scrolls.
For those who choose Torah scrolls, try choosing human beings.
For those who choose humanity, try choosing divinity.
For those who choose divinity, try choosing humanity.
Turn, turn, and return.
Come full circle in law and life.

Here we stand,
Daughters and sons of Abraham.
But are we bound to the same grave fate?
Hands tied and face to face with our parent's blade?
With only the angels and our own blind obedience to save us
    from demise.
We were so young and unknowing at the time.
Oh, G-d of wounded children, custodian of the anguished's cries,
Shelter us.
Assure us.
That there is no leap of faith, let alone no gesture of loyalty
    so great, that it outweighs the sting of our tears and the
    recognition of our pain.
Allow us to find a better meaning, a fuller meaning of Torah's
    words in which children are not only seen but heard.
And as we seek meaning from our tradition, may we release
    the binds of old stories, redeeming Isaac and redeeming
    ourselves.
Amen.

PART 2

DANIEL AT THE WINDOW

When the world was breaking
And so was he,
Daniel found the nearest window,
Looked outside,
Drew a map to the East of his heart,
And prayed.

His prayer did not alter the wreckage,
Mollify G-d, or stop the breaking.
But it moved him to utter the words
That would become the paths of future generations.

As we seek the center
And the land of our heart's content
Allow us to see that our maps become other people's
     compasses
Our selves become other people's starting places.
And our footprints become the passageways that eventually
Somewhere
Some way
Lead our People, and us,

Home.

What is it like to not pray?
A dove without wings.
A lute without strings.
And a sky without stars.

The *midbar* is my mouth.
When it opens, there is nothing
But dryness and dull aching.

But there is something forming.
A flood rising in the dark of my lungs.

The tide, she whispers:

רוּחַ חַיִּים

The spirit
Moves here.
Quiet and dampened.
But alas.

She lives.

A ballad of Hannah.
Not G-d's favorite.
But the toiling other
Who spoke of cooption
And evil so commonplace
It rose with the sun to meet us on our way to work
And with the moon to lull us to sleep in our beds.
This Hannah was not weeping.
But writing and gasping.
For while others walked and talked in a circle
She walked to the outer limit
And, in outrage, took out her pen
And drew her own path far from home.

I confess.
I, son of David,
Am not deep in knowing
Or slight in anger.

For mine is a body of fools,
A mind that is neither world wise nor heaven sent
And a heart that cannot and will disguise its rage.

Torah's ink has seeped through my fingers,
Staining my bones with the soil of memory and pain.

I cannot form words or letters.
I can only fall further until pitch-black becomes me.

Permit my pen to command the ink
To tell the truth
To transmit the story
To temper that which now flows through me.

And, with your steady hand, can finally be brought onto the
    parchment and into the light.

I have visions.
But they aren't of G-d.

There are fangs, ribs, and teeth.
Unutterable sounds that talk only in the nighttime.

Why they choose to whisper to me, I cannot conceive!

Let me heed not the unholy.
And turn away from the company of idols and kings.

And though I do not have pronouncements
Grant me the continued grace of the glimpsing.

For does this world not need the kind of quiet seeing that lets
G-d and the generations cry out and speak?

Miriam, you are rooted in the bitterness of tears.
And yet you are the one who returned us to the majesty of the
    sea
The softness of sand
And the power of dance.

You revealed that we, like our names, belong to this world.
And we do not.

And so, we must rise heavenward and remain earth-bound in
    the abundance of our joy and the search for freedom that
    does not end.

I am not the book
Or even the page.
The arm outstretched
Or the grass that fades.

I am a desert bereft of metaphor.
There is only sand.
But during the night and in the day
The moon and sun come out to greet me.
And I know, despite the wilderness, I am never truly alone.

There is a blessing to honor your parents.
But is there a blessing to be angry at them?
The Rambam tells us to avoid anger.
But was he there when Joseph's brothers sold him into slavery?
When Hagar and child were cast out of her husband's house?
When Shem and Japeth covered Noah, naked and drunk?
To choose not to sin, yes.
But to disregard the sins of others, no.
Never.

G-d requires something more.
To face others and ourselves.
To see when others are wickedly or unwittingly blind.
This is where Rambam, Almighty G-d, and we all must meet.
In the moment when we could look away
But decide instead to look closer and say
Not in G-d's name.
And certainly not in ours.

Barukh Dayan Ha'emet.
Blessed is the True Judge.

This is a blessing
For hands shaking
Nerves frightfully twitching
And a heartrending at the appointment you just didn't want to
take.
It would have been easier to refuse the day, to make excuses, to
run far away from the reality and far away from here.
But not you, dear Heart: You stayed.
You walked out the door and into the next room. And with
your feet planted firmly. And the millions of tiny heartbeats
and all your generations there, quietly, supporting...
You pulled up a chair at the doctor's office and leapt.

I missed the *kiddush*.
And the *kedusha*, too.
For these days, I separate myself from community
In the waiting room of my own private *oneg*.

How can I dress the Torah when I can barely dress myself?
How can I make the matzoh ball soup when I have forgotten
    the recipe?

Sit with me in the room.
And walk me, when I am ready, out the door.

And bless these steps and this heart.
Pilgrim, on the path of the ancestors.
Unarrived but on the great journey still.

I have seen the narrow place
Where beauty is broken.
And redemption floats like Moshe in the basket along the
River Fate.
Here, the tearful triumphs,
The destitute prospers.
And the beggar becomes the giver of the whole world.
Here, G-d's words flow from the narrowness
And the prophet is disguised as a human being,
Quietly creating the passageways that lead us to freedom's
mighty sea.

For those of us searching for fathers who never show
May we find it in our heart of hearts
To cling, still.
And may we find Ruth's loving embrace
In our teachers,
In our neighbors,
In all people who nurse our broken pieces.
And when we are both famished and alone
May G-d grant us the peace of knowing valiant women
Who, with the height of the tallest wheat field,
Feed the hungering depths of our seeking souls.

Our performance is not the great reveal.
And despite the act ongoing
And the audience applauding
We are still behind the curtain
Shaking
Wondering
When we get to be who we really are.

"When" is not the moment of Jacob's gifts.
Or angels that are delusions of grandeur or pity.

But Esau.

The hidden brother, red and screaming.

Holy is the mystery of the unseen.
And a seeing that gives up the fantasy of what we appear to be
    and how others appear to us.

3.

MIRIAM IN THE BULRUSHES

A sadness unlike Hannah wailing
Or bottled tears of worn out travelers in the psalms
A sadness that precedes deliverance
That troubles the senses like a muddled fog
Confusing us and making us yearn for the sight of what comes
    after
(Clouds of glory, not clouds of obstruction,
Please, G-d).
May we demystify the fog,
Go out in search of that place "afar off"
Like Abraham.
And with the promise of Shekhinah
Seek out the mountain where G-d does dwell.
And where neither cloud cover
Nor the mortal haze of human beings
Masks the certainty of the way forward.

My womb is not the well
That draws out the water
That gives you life.

And I am not the daughter who fills your pitcher.

I refuse to be what I do for you.
And I refuse to be the shadow of what you do to me.

I am larger than all the vessels you try to contain me in.

And though my face is hidden
I am the Glory

Greater than glances,
Bigger than bodies, and

More revealing than sight.

I have a name but too often I have been rendered nameless.
Me too.
I have a voice but too often my voice has not been heeded.
Me too.
I have a shape but too often my body has been leered at or
    made invisible.
Me too.
All these acts.
To make a person.
This person
Disappear.
And yet.
I have a name
And a voice
And a body.
Together, in the midst of the others, I make myself present and
    available for all survivors and our collective surviving.
Me too.
Me too.
And
Me too.

The song of Abishag
Is a ballad of our great illusion.
For in the lines formed by the sharp curve of our retinas
We missed the soft and hidden words of her own telling.
We must bury ourselves in text.
To the point where we see not with the sight of a noble king or
    even matriarchs fair.
But until we dig so deep, the light goes out.
And all we are left with is the truth of Torah dark.
G-d of all generations,
Reveal to us the voiceless and the real.
And give to us not eyes that see
But hearts that feel
For the silent stories,
All the hidden beauties masked by our own obscurity
But waiting
Between the lines
To be revealed.

In the presence of G-d, Sarah Emainu sat scoffing but secretly
    fearing:
"Do I deserve the good?
And the grace-filled?
And the life-giving?"
And although she bore life, she is remembered to have laughed
    coldly in its face.
But what if her jeer was her coping?
And her knowing?
And her humanity?
We, who greet the miracles amidst the bitterness and the real.
We are like Sarah.
Mother to curiosity.
Mother to doubt.
Mother to the scholar and the Dairy Man.
Mother to the generations of women who question the world
    and, too, the Word.

How do we turn to a text
That people have used like the twist of their backs
To turn away from total strangers?
And how do we turn to a People
Who have put a fence around tradition designed to keep
    others out?

For those of us who have dared look closer
Run the risk of becoming pillars of salt with our questions
Or being swallowed in some pit of the earth for our rebellions.

Encourage us to plead, like Abraham, against any and all
    destruction,
Especially in Torah's name.
And lead us to speak up
For the sake of all the living and the dead.

We may be dust and ashes
But our lives are worth something.
And our disagreement is worth everything.

Here are the words that are never written
That kick up the dust we unknowingly sit in.

The shtetl dweller is secretly a Hasid.

For the fixer knows the value of making.
Busy hands. A constant tailoring.

All these years our soul craft has patched up the world and, in
every age, stopped its breaking.

The vessels shook
And the lights burst forth.

Far below, they traveled
Into the most sturdy and unsuspecting hearts.
And the humans kept the lights hidden
So they could survive carefully in the looming dark.
But despite pogroms,
Then pushkas
Then ploughshares
Recurring Pharoahs and Josephs gritting their teeth so hard,
The fight to just be nearly broke them.
None of us ever did bend the knee.
We just had to learn to find our lights.
And become.

אהיה אשר אהיה

אהיה אשר אהיה

They ask.
They always ask.
And I
With trepidation
And trembling
Must give them the answer I know they do not want.

So, I search myself
Going past the puppetry
And the bag of answers labeled "Theirs"
Into the furthest corner of myself.

And there I sit.
Drawing out the words that call to me in this place.
And in one hard push they come through me and fall one by
   one out of my mouth.

"I am okay.
Yes, I am just right, really.
Even when I can't."

You concealed yourself
When our wickedness triumphed.

And some say,
You looked away whenever wickedness triumphed over us.

I say, you peeked through divine hands
And with divine eyes
Caught glimpses of our persistent goodness.
So that when you withdrew you also came close.

Handing us Your words. Dressing us in Your truths.
True, we still shroud You in mystery.
But you are always nearby.

Barukh atah Adonai eloheinu melekh ha-olam asher kidshanu
b'mitzvotav v'tzivanu la'asok b'divrei Torah.

G-d of our ancestors, allow me through study to bring what is
seen into hiding and what is hidden into plain sight.

To encounter You and Your revelation, and to know Your
mystery. Amen.

Speechless space dweller,
Are you still in the synagogues and study houses?
Or in the silences that do not utter your name?
Do you still reveal yourself in minyan?
Or do you unmask in the quiet corners and unfamiliar streets
    of our own hidden longing?
For once, do not lead me.
But come to me.
This solitary party.
This congregation of one.
Find me in the emptying,
In the absence of clutter and noise.
Make yourself known to me.
And as you enter my home,
Know I will exit,
Making that long trek yonder
To yours.

Lo! Your Genesis.

Like darkness that lingered over the deep, you were cloaked in
    shadow but still empty.

Eager for form but lacking in self-made meaning,

You placed yourself within someone else's fence.
It was only natural,
You thought at the time.
But the thought nagged at you and teased you.
"Whose garden?"
So, one day, you mustered up the courage to leave.

Though at times, you felt your uncertainty could drown you.
Neither water nor earth could contain you
For you are and have always been the sky.

There is no fence to keep you in.
There is only vast expansiveness for you to begin again and
    again and again.
I found my joy.
She wasn't hiding.
She was waiting.
For the moment to lean forward,
To come from the middle of my chest,
Open up my throat.
And laugh without holding back.

הִגְדִּיל יְהוָה, לַעֲשׂוֹת עִמָּנוּ
הָיִינוּ שְׂמֵחִים

"The Lord will do great things for us and we shall rejoice."

Akiva was a shepherd.

Rambam was a physician.

And women whose names we may never utter
Have been life carriers in ways that transcended the fog of
tradition and time.

Some, before they were Rabbis.

Some, while they were Rabbis.

But all of them stitched their being into becoming Rabbis.

This is what I tell myself when I stare into the mystery:

What is beyond us is embedded deep within us.

We can, through this work, here, join ourselves to what lies far
out there.

And when the way becomes lost to us,

Or we become lost to the way,

We can remember:

We are travelers on the path our ancestors took.

Alone is an illusion.

And the company we keep is as old as the world.

Memory is the eternal vital sign.
And life? A persistent breath.

Sometimes, gasping.
But also, exhaling.
Letting out the vitality we hold inside.

There are maimings and then killings.
"What comes from us lasts long after us."
Or so it is often said.

But we mustn't forget.
Lives are meant for living.
And the breath of life can outlast even senseless death.

וַיֹּאמֶר אֵלַי, הִנָּבֵא עַל-הָעֲצָמוֹת הָאֵלֶּה; וְאָמַרְתָּ אֲלֵיהֶם הָעֲצָמוֹת
הַיְבֵשׁוֹת, שִׁמְעוּ דְּבַר-יְהוָה
כֹּה אָמַר אֲדֹנָי יְהוִה לָעֲצָמוֹת הָאֵלֶּה הִנֵּה
אֲנִי מֵבִיא בָכֶם רוּחַ וִחְיִיתֶם
וְנָתַתִּי עֲלֵיכֶם גִּדִים וְהַעֲלֵתִי עֲלֵיכֶם בָּשָׂר
וְקָרַמְתִּי עֲלֵיכֶם עוֹר וְנָתַתִּי בָכֶם רוּחַ וִחְיִיתֶם
וִידַעְתֶּם כִּי אֲנִי יְהוָה

So says the Lord G-d to these bones; Behold, I will cause spirit
to enter into you, and you shall live!

And I will lay sinews upon you, and I will make flesh grow
over you and cover you with skin and put breath into you,

and you will live, and you will then know that I am the Lord.

The space between remembrance and redemption is best filled with falling.

Falling away from a past that can strangle us with its *tzitzit*.
And falling into the soft fabric of our own choosing,
In which every act draws us closer to the Source
And wraps us in the embrace of nurturing and whole-making
Jewish lives.

בָּרוּךְ אַתָּה ה' אֱלֹהֵינוּ, מֶלֶךְ הָעוֹלָם אֲשֶׁר קִדְּשָׁנוּ בְּמִצְוֹתָיו וְצִוָּנוּ עַל מִצְוַת צִיצַת

Blessed are you, Creator of the Universe, who commands us to study our fringes and fashion our communities like prayer shawls, that they grow to inclusively shelter all people.

Fear not.
For one day, prayer will leap joyously again from your lips.
The words, of course.
And, too, the sway.
And the mystery
And the silence speckled with hope-dust rising through the air.
In the meantime, know that the beginning
And even redemption
Were only made possible by the time in between.
Time like the days you spend now.
For without the interim creation days, *olam hazeh* and *olam
haba* would have never come to be.
Yes. The unfinished is holy.
And the absent. And the moving.
These are the primary experiences of being human.
And the primary building blocks of heaven and earth.

Somewhere between the stirrups and the paper nightgown
   clinging to my body,
My soul ascended mid-air like an artist on a trapeze

Unsure where to grab hold.
On the one end children, birthday parties, and ice cream.
And on the other, withered eggshells.
Cast away from the last Passover *seder*.
(Does the plague of the firstborn move in my body, still?)

The doctor talked so casually of my desert
And so definitely of my future.
That all I've known since then is bondage.
The shackles of what other people tell me about my body.
And the prison populated by the lie that led me here; that I am
   a plague and no longer, life.

Ha-Kadosh Barukh Hu,
Help me see myself as you do.
To walk faithfully in your Image.
Filled with movement and the spirit of the living.

Lead me back to myself.
And to the ancient Promise you bequeathed our People.
Then, back to you.

So the soul that once dared on the trapeze
Can at last let her arms go
And dare bravely to come back to life.
Come back to You.

Who is the witness that will see and hear you?
Will she sit by the window sill?
Or will she walk up close to listen?
In the place between what you observe and remember
What people told you and what you know within yourself to
  be true
May you find that the witness you are seeking
She exists and is waiting patiently in you.

When did humility become synonymous with submission?

And knowledge synonymous with grandeur?

Are we not to gather firewood to warm others, rather than
ourselves?

Can we not nurture our soul's fire and submit to something
greater still?

G-d of our ancestors,

Set our hearts aflame.

But walk us on paths that tread cautiously.

That we may learn as we teach.

And teach as we learn.

Knowing the power of the flame but taking special care never
to inflict a burn.

The Apocrypha tells us that ten tribes of Israel were lost.
Or rather, stolen.
Carted and carried along the narrow places of the Euphrates
River.
And we were held captive by foreign masters.
And the hope of being made numerous like the stars of heaven.
But instead of stars, we were seeds.
Transplants of Yosef.
Sold into slavery and then rising from the ground to feed the
hungry and welcome back our kin.
Narrowness has been our passage.
And we have been made small and broken by the way.
But our scattering has seeded our return.
For as we have turned to the world
We, too, have returned to ourselves.
Building a New Eden
Rooted in the wholeness of our shared humanity
And the radical tending to every human being living on the Earth.

Lo, my seasons of no gathering, leaves shedding or land emptying.

There are seeds.

But there is no water.

Only hopelessness and longing.

G-d, lift the *shloshim* of my heart.

Not this season of loss.

By my inability to lift the veil and see:

For human life is not the longest wheat field, or the planted
  things patiently waiting,

But the paths of our ancestors, who join us in our waiting.

Sarah, cursing and laughing.

Hagar, with thirst still yearning.

Miriam, without timbrel or dancing.

And Hannah, ceaseless and crying.

Adonai, sow within me the knowing:

That my grief is in great company.

And I?

I am with the ancestors.

They are always close by.

And I am never

Not ever

Alone.

When I imagine peace
I imagine the world shaking.
And our ancestors gathering in the ancient academies of
    Jewish learning.
And in the midst of wailing ... a pause for creating.
Then, the words of Oseh Shalom and Kaddish Yatom emerging
    like holy lights enkindling the room
And repairing the breach.
As they lamented their oppression
And envisioned their long-sought-after liberation.
They imparted to every generation:
Peace does not occur in the happy places.
It is the bursting of Jewish light.
Into our millennia-long rebellion against the intruding and
    lingering dark.

I can see you up close and from miles away.
Through dozens of near ones and even perfect strangers
But ever the same stern pair of eyes.
And you look at me.
And tug at me.
And manipulate me.
And each time, I reveal your guise.

I have pretended
I did not know.
But I have always
In fact known.

Today, I made it past your altar.
Shielded myself from your gaze.
And stumbled into the divine wilderness of the unseen.

In this Holy of Holies,
G-d and I.
Come
At last
To meet.

פנים אל פנים

For the first time.
Face to face.

There is an invisible staff we carry.

Passed from Jacob during the time of his wrestling,
To Aaron as he gestured in faithful summoning,
Calling upon G-d's wonders to lead us to freedom at the sea.

The staff is our certainty,
Our history and destiny.
To make our ancestors' dreams and all our dreams, living, here
    today.
Neither the force of angels nor the hardened heart of Pharaoh
    could ever halt its passing through the generations.

By the staff, we know that our redemption is not only possible
But palpable, burned into memory, and real.

From the staff we behold the most precious of all Jewish
    continuities:
That our ancestors, like our future, exist within us.

What is a soul?
Is it united with the body or separate?
Is it perfected or a work in progress?
What of a Jewish soul?
Does our essence carry our generations?
Does a Jewish mother preside over her child's soul?

Hers was a motherhood of laughter and photo albums.
Yours was a childhood in which children were not to be heard
or seen.
Hers was a motherhood of fierce love against all odds.
Yours was a childhood in which you were the odd one out.
Hers was a motherhood of selflessness and sacrifice.
Yours was a childhood in which to have a self was the ultimate
betrayal.

For years, you have been telling yourself that yours is hers.
That she and you are inescapably bound in the same glad tale.

And yet here you stand, open to the truth of your own existence.
Your one, individual life in the midst of all that forced sharing.

You know what's true.
And anyway, she can be herself and you can be you.

O, Source of Life:
Grant me clarity of mind and body to know the truth of my
own soul.

4.

MOSES' MOMENT OF LIFE/DEATH

What of the scratch that does not fade?
A mark not of the covenant
But of the fracture.

How our face turned white at the sight of the bush that burned.
And how the rock cracked us open, inconsolable and raging.

May what ages us
And breaks us
Not bury us
But rise within us
So we may meet G-d and Israel
Ever-living
And true.

"Moshe was a hundred and twenty years old when he died; his
    eyes were undimmed and his vigor unabated"

May the traumas, losses, and changes be the signs of our
    awakeness and that we have truly lived.

At last, after all the years apart,
The gulf between us filled with yells and silent misgivings,
I have decided to understand
What formed you.
What pressed upon you.
To behold you as layers of crust in the Earth
Whose rocks build up and erode over time
(How are we to determine the source?)
I pour my nutrients
And my health into you and your many layers.
And for the first time in both our lives,
I give you the love you could not give me.

Barukh atah Adonai, eloheinu melekh ha-olam, she-asani b'tzelem
Elohim.
Blessed are you Adonai, our God, sovereign of the universe,
who made me in the image of God.

Love is not the possession of commandments of stone
Or a lover's banner dangling pleasingly upon the skin,
But the moment after the last song is sung
And all the wine has all been drunk,
When only woundedness
And the revelation of a prolonged aching keep us company.
Love lives here.
Unmasking and detaching
And for once, abandoning the sweetness of illusion
For the bitter release of the truth.

That first dance.
No, not the one at your wedding.
Or even the first time you felt your hips move on their own
and sway.
But the time you chose to leave your fear and your room.
To do away with "you must make your bed and lie in it."
Something inside of you moved.
The backbeat of your soul became a melody that ignited love
and limb.
And soon, every part of you was back in the circle,
doing *hakafot* of the heart with your People.

G-d, remind me.
Of this moment.
Of this body.
Of this joy.

So when I am once again laid down by life, I can raise myself
in this dance of boundless, unmitigated joy.

What does it take to turn mourning to dancing?
First, a reaching forward.
A subtle movement out of the slump of our *shiva* chair (not
    quite upright, but still).

Then, the planting of our feet on the ground.
"Yes," we are here and grounded in the roots of divine justice.
It is now possible to stand.

Though the whispers of fate and even the Angel of Death
Tell us to stay a while.
To reject words of consolation for the heaviness of our sorrow.
Though they would have us look away from ourselves and all life,
We face the dark.

And somewhere, a prism of light forms.
We can barely make it out.
But when our vision and we, too, are ready
We see it as bright as day:

"Arise."

Arise in the presence of friends.
Arise and leave behind the tear and the tearing.
Arise and make those first few steps among the living.

And though we stand up and sit down,
Agonize over what we are able to do and not do,
Individual acts of mind, body, and soul

Will lead us to give up the grief and ignite our dry bones.

And one of these days, when we least expect it, we will find
ourselves dancing.

These are the words no one tells you.
Buried beneath the tomb of the patriarchs
And the last wall left standing.
And the village stained with our ancestor's blood
Now covered in daffodils.
We fall apart.
The ones back there, and us, here.
Underneath the weight of silence and racism.
And singing our strength's praises.
We fall apart.
Though we have relished our survival
We mustn't ever forget our tears.
Buried in the ground we find a story shrouded in secrecy.
The ruins have become our living.
And yet, a new Eden calls to us there,
Urging us to draw forth life from the memory of death.

This fence around Torah.
Can women and children peak through?
Is there a door for doubters and strangers?
A way in for the serially abused?
Is its wood beige and blended in?
Or from trees with roots of many different accents and hints?

True, the fence was first meant to keep us in.
The People who fell easily to idols.

Whose stiff-neck led us into wilderness and sin.

And yet, the fence was broken
To invite the poor into the sukkah
Servants into the field
And G-d, out, into the world.

The gulf between judgment and protection is best filled by
    human beings
Who paint the fence,
Take up the fence.
And through their work and being renew Torah.

My joy is not
Sunset
Serendipity
The tallest height
Or the ripest tree
But, rather, a presence that bursts forth from the emptiness.
Unconcerned about the fill of my cup
And committed to being a blessing
That grows and pushes up through the cracks,
Every single day.

Today, amidst scorn, I wept.
And when the last jeer was dealt,
I opened my mouth.
And behold, praise!
Oceans of praise pouring out.

I am the desert flower that bloomed,
Pushing up against sand and death,
Growing the earth with plentiful cries.
Although I fear I have nothing left.

The days of Israel's prophets and kings have long past
Yet are possible even now.
For fruits of justice and fearlessness do arise
When mothers' tears (my tears) become as seeds in the ground.

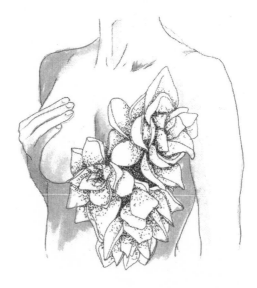

No is the one who left the building
And the community
Before Yes was first proposed and No was disinvited from the
    party.

No is the unexpected death.
Act 7, Scene 3.
Yes leapt from a balcony.
And amidst the blood and the breaking
No was defiantly, creatively born,
Screaming.

No is that spontaneous combustion.
A woman's first magic trick.
Inside the home.
Inside the Book.
Inside herself.
So she could waltz in when everyone least expected her,
And cha-cha to her first solo dance of creative destruction.

What falls apart
Cannot be put back together.

But when the sameness crumbles
Creation peaks through.

Daring us.
Daring you.

To reveal your uniqueness.
To remove your shell.

And make your inside
Out.

No, you will never be the same.

But becoming always does triumph holding.

Because when you let go of the old pieces,
You fall purposefully into who you are meant to be.

Here is the secret that burns through the flame, survives the
    flood, and outlasts the grave:
We are made out of Heaven and Earth.
All this time.
And for all time.
The universe has been Us.

A psalm of evolution.
We were not born merely to survive
But thrive.
Because though we were forged in the persistent bonds of tiny
    molecules
We still belong.
To a ground that holds us long after our bodies fade away.
We are out-living life.
Transcending death.
And ours is the blossoming of an endless becoming.

There is a space
Beyond guilt
And struggle
And shame.
The space where the ladder ends.
And we all begin.

The climb, though necessary,
Is not worth everything.

And that which is worth everything is more precious than even
the highest rung.

G-d shelters and reveals in the unknown.
When we stop pushing and start embracing, we will finally
find ourselves on holy ground.

Artisan,
We need your art
And your shadow
And your unknowing
And your hands to rebuild the tabernacle.
We do not need a structure of jewels and ornaments.
Or liberators that come to us by noble or anointed births.
We just need the wisdom that rebuffs prophets.
And a movable place so flexible and centered it fills the
    wilderness with G-d's glory.
Holding us in motion and widening our souls to the expanse of
    the heavens above and our limitless imagination below.
We need a new blessing.
A blessing for Bezalel.
And even more, Artist?
We need the blessing of you.

Are there truly two Jerusalems?

And what if the so-called Other is an imagining of our
   ancestor?

A lingering in the shadows of your Great Mountain?

Adonai yireh
Maybe G-d did forsee
That instead of I and You
There has been
And there remains
Only
Us.

Our opposites like our forced peace will break us.
But the remembrance that we come from
Each Other
Will provide for all of us.
In all our days on this Earth.

And beyond.

I came so long
And so far.
And yet all I can do is stand here planted at the shores of the sea.
Is my life worth nothing when I am standing still?
Looking out into the further and with the memory of all that
life back there?
Redemption's road is winding, waiting.
Calling me home but not quite yet.
Because in this year of my birth, I am, for the first time, awake
and not asleep.
And when I stare into life,
This time, I won't ever forget.

I was never a scholar
Or a farmer
Or even a store keeper.

But I clung to each as if they were the Word.

Not knowing that my words flowed like lightning from my
    fingertips.

Animating each calling with the electricity of a thousand clap
    backs.

Against the weight of generations
And encircling them, still,

In old yearning and crisp vigor,
Ever writing our story of the ages.

I did not fall apart
To be put back together.

So I could come back to the field
And, come spring, collect a handsome bushel.

I let myself drip in pain.
So I could arrive at the next winter
Bruised
Bandaged and
Basket empty.

Knowing that my broken pieces were roots
Planted deep for generations who will sit in my place and seek
    out sadness's fruit.

I was in the wilderness.
You couldn't tell at the time.

The sand dunes were as heavy as my silences.
Far gone from my destination, I pretended that I arrived.

But the walking kept me from disappearing
And the weeping became the well from which I drew my healing.

Not all at once.
A few gradual sips of the sunrise.

Drinking in the colors, distance, and vision,
The notion that every sunset is followed by this beginning.

But that's still not a reason to wander.
Being lost taught me to linger

And that every single moment is worth more than forever.
Aimless steps stretch out time.

Reminding us that our desert thirst is worth more than the
    mythic homes we set out for.
And to walk is greater than to grasp.

NOTES

All biblical translations are from the JPS Tanakh (2000). All talmudic references are from the Babylonian Talmud.

Part 1

<small>PAGE 3</small>
The Quote Verifier: Who Said What, Where, and When, Ralph Keyes, p. 159
Proverbs 24:4
Anatomy of the Soul, Yitzchak Ginsburgh, point 19 on p. 120

<small>PAGE 4</small>
Genesis 9:21–28
Genesis 10

<small>PAGE 5</small>
Genesis 32:22–31

<small>PAGE 6</small>
Exodus 1
Pesikta Rabbati 43

<small>PAGE 7</small>
Genesis 25:22

<small>PAGE 8</small>
Lamentations Rabbah, chs. 1–5.
See also: *Jeremiah Interpreted: A Rabbinic Analysis of the Prophet*, Bryna Jocheved Levy, pp. 10–25

PAGE 10
Exodus 2–3:14

PAGE 11
Genesis 12:4
Numbers 20:11–12

PAGE 12
Genesis Rabbah 38:13
The Talmud: Selected Writings, edited by Ben Zion Bokser,
    Baruch M. Bokser, p. 76
See Rav Samuel b. Nahmani
1 Kings 3:11–12
Numbers 32:13
Exodus 2:3–4

PAGE 14
Be'ur Eser S'firot, Azriel of Geronia, Section 2

PAGE 15
1 Kings 19:16
Exodus 3:2

PAGES 18–19
A Heart Afire: Stories and Teachings of the Early Hasidic Masters,
    Translated and Retold with Commentary by Zalman
    Schachter Shalomi and Netanel Miles-Yepez, pp. 7–8

Ecclesiastes 2: 12–16

Daniel 7:5

A *Feminist Companion to Exodus to Deuteronomy*, edited by
Athalya Brenner-Idan, p. 116.
Exodus 15:20

The Jewish Study Bible (2004), pp. 1–7.
Talmudic Stories: Narrative Art, Composition, and Culture,
Jeffrey L. Rubenstein, p. 123
Exodus 6:6
Psalm 37:2
Ezekiel 29:5

Mishneh Torah, Maimonides, Sefer Madda, Human
Dispositions, chapter 1, paragraph 4
Genesis 37:27
Genesis 21:14
Genesis 9:23
Babylonian Talmud, Berachot 54a

The New Jewish Encyclopedia, edited by David Bridger and

Samuel Wolk, pp. 78, 417, 182, 86

The Cambridge History of Judaism: Volume 4, The Late Roman-Rabbinic Period, p. 767 (See: footnote #36 on evolution and significance of *kedushot* in Jewish prayer)

PAGE 38
Strong's Exhaustive Concordance of the Bible, p. 1532
Exodus 2:3
Tales of Elijah the Prophet, Peninnah Schram, p. xxxi
Exodus 15:1–18

PAGE 39
Ruth 1:16, 2:23

PAGE 41
Genesis 25:5, 33:10–11, 25:22, 25:25, 27:41

Part 3
PAGE 44
1 Samuel 1:10
Psalm 56:8
Genesis 15:13
Exodus 13:21, 14:24
Genesis 22:4
Exodus 24:16

PAGE 45
Genesis 24:17–19, 34:1–2

Zohar II 42b, 163b
Exodus 13:20–22

PAGE 48
1 Kings 1:1–4

PAGE 49
Genesis 18:12
Makkot 24b
Tevye the Dairyman and the Railroad Stories, Sholem Aleichem, in
particular, "Chava," 69–82

PAGE 50
Pirke Avot, 2:1
Genesis 19:26
Numbers 16:32
Genesis 18:23–32, 3:9
Job 39:19
Pirke Avot 5:17

PAGE 52
A Heart Afire, p. 8

PAGE 53
*From Metaphysics to Midrash: Myth, History and the
Interpretation of Scripture in Lurianic Kabbala*, Shaul Magid,
pp. 22–23
Pogroms: Anti-Jewish Violence in Modern Russian History, John
Doyle Klier and Shlomo Lambroza

The Jewish Experience, Fishburn Books, p. 30
A Village by the Jordan: The Story of Degania, Joseph Baratz
Exodus 1:8
2 Kings 16
Genesis 42:6
Psalm 119:130
Exodus 3:14

PAGE 56

Genesis 3:10, 3:14, 3:23–24
Jewish Liturgy as a Spiritual System: A Prayer-By-Prayer Explanation of the Nature and Meaning of Jewish Worship, Arnold S. Rosenberg, pp. 41–42
Space and Place in Jewish Studies, Barbara E. Mann, pp. 11–15

PAGE 57

Space and Place in Jewish Studies, Barbara E. Mann, pp. 81–97

PAGE 59

Genesis 1:2, 7–8, 3:23–24

PAGE 60

Solomon and the Ant and Other Jewish Folktales, retold by Sheldon Oberman, p. 45
Medicine in the Mishneh Torah of Maimonides, Fred Rosner

PAGES 62–64

Ezekiel 37:4–6
New York Times, Letter to the Editor, Rabbi Gilbert S. Rosenthal, September 19, 2013 (paraphrasing the Ba'al

Shem Tov based on Rabbi Gilbert S. Rosenthal's rendering
of this quote)
*Ha-Siddur Ha-Shalem: Siddur Ashkenaz, Weekday Shacharit,
Preparatory Prayers* (found at Sefaria.org)
Numbers 15:37
Psalm 100

PAGE 65
Genesis 1
Pirke Avot 4:21

PAGE 66
Shulchan Arukh, Orakh Chayim 476:2
The JPS Dictionary of Jewish Words, Joyce Eisenberg and Ellen
Scolnic, pp. 52, 56

PAGE 67
Elie Wiesel and the Art of Storytelling, Rosemary Horowitz, p. 29

PAGE 68
A Code of Jewish Ethics, Volume 2, Joseph Telushkin, p. 224
(see description of Rabbi Elijah Chaim Meisel)
*Midrash Tanhuma-Yelammedenu: An English Translation of
Genesis and Exodus from the printed version of Tanhuma-
Yelammedenu with an Introduction, Notes and Indexes*, pp.
332–333

PAGE 69
2 Esdras 13:40–45

The Forging of Races: Race and Scripture in the Protestant
Atlantic World, Colin Kidd, pp. 1600–2000, 43

PAGE 70
Exodus 23:11
Moed Katan 21b
Genesis 21:9–10, 18:12, 21:15–16
Numbers 12:10
1 Samuel 1:10

PAGE 71
Folktales of the Jews, Volume 2: Tales from Eastern Europe, Dan
Ben-Amos and Dov Noy, pp. 15–19

PAGE 73
Hakdamat Sefer-Ha Zohar, 1:10b, 11a
Genesis 22:13, 19, 26:23–25
Exodus 40:34, 33:11

PAGE 74
Genesis 32:25
Exodus 7:8–10
Jewish Encyclopedia, 1906, entry by: J. Frederic McCurdy and
    Louis Ginzberg (online at: http://www.jewishencyclopedia.
    com/articles/5-aaron-s-rod)

Part 4
PAGE 78
Exodus 34:29

Numbers 20:11
Deuteronomy 34:7

PAGE 79
Mishkan T'filah: Services for Shabbat; a Reform Siddur, p. 84

PAGE 81
Exodus 20:1–14
Song of Solomon 2:4

PAGE 82
Kitzur Shulchan Arukh 138:7
Mishnah Brurah 669:11

PAGES 83–84
Psalm 30:11
Psalm 31:12
Exodus 12:23
Numbers 21:17
Wrestling with the Angel: Insights on Death and Mourning, Jack
    Riemer, p. 164
Ezekiel 37:1–7
Ecclesiastes 3:4

PAGE 85
Vilna Gaon's Letter to the Lost Tribes of Israel, paragraph 20
Midrash Tehilim 11:4, Rabbi Mike Feuer, Jerusalem Anthology
*Neighbors: The Destruction of the Jewish Community in Jedwabne
    Poland*, Jan Tomasz Gross

A Village Names Dowgalishok: The Massacre at Radun and Eishishok, Avraham Av'iel
Judaism when Christianity Began: A Survey of Belief and Practice, Jacob Neusner, p. 136

PAGE 86
Pirke Avot 1:1
Pirke Avot 3:2
Exodus 32:1–6
Deuteronomy 29:16
Exodus 33:3
Mishneh Torah, Yom Tov, 6:18
Rabbi Shlomo Riskin's retelling of a Levi Yitzchak of Berdichev tale
Leviticus 23:22
Deuteronomy 15:12–14

PAGE 87
Psalm 113:3
Megillat Esther
Genesis 11:4
Nahum 3:12
Psalm 23:5
Song of Solomon 2:14

PAGE 89
1 Samuel 1:10, 12–13
Poem #67
Exodus 15:20–21

PAGE 91
Genesis 9:8

PAGE 93
Hannah Senesh: Her Life and Diary, The First Complete Edition,
    p. 306
Shulchan Arukh, Orach Chayim, 580:2
Genesis 8:15–16, 1:27
Bereishit Rabbah 17:4

PAGE 94
Daniel 12:2
Avodah Zarah 5a

PAGE 95
Genesis 28:12
Radak on Genesis 28:13

PAGE 97
Exodus 35:30–34
*The Alef-beit: Jewish Thought Revealed through the Hebrew
    Letters,* Yitshak Ginzburg, Avraham Arieh Trugman, and
    Moshe Yaakov Wisnefsky, pp. 7
Exodus 36:1
Kol Dodi Sofek, Job 6, Joseph B. Soloveitchik, translated by
    David Z. Gordon (2006)
*Samuel and the Deuteronomist: A Literary Study of the
    Deuteronomic History, Part 2: 1 Samuel,* Robert Polzin
Exodus 40:34–38

Berakhot 55a:11
Midrash Tanchuma, Vayakhel 1:2

PAGE 98
*Righteous Gentiles in the Hebrew Bible: Ancient Role Models for
Sacred Relationships,* Rabbi Jeffrey K. Salkin, pp. 8–9

PAGE 99
Exodus 15:21
Tosefta Softa 6:1

PAGE 100
Tevye the Dairyman and the Railroad Stories, by Sholem
   Aleichem
*The Letters of Menakhem-Mendl and Sheyne-Sheyndl, and
   Motl, the Cantor's Son,*
Sholem Aleichem

PAGE 101
Leviticus 25:1–7
Introduction to the Mishnah, Maimonides, 17:14

PAGE 102
Exodus 14:13
Eruvin 54a:24

ACKNOWLEDGMENTS

To all those who fling out compassion like *b'nei mitzvah* candy and whose expansive lives make real the vision of this book: April N. Baskin, Dr. Tarece Johnson, Rabbi Julia Watts Belser, Dr. Cynthia Levine-Rasky, David Karpel, Rachel Kann, Elad Nehorai, Rabbi Jill Zimmerman, Rabbi Sharon Brous, Rabbi Michael Adam Latz, Cantor Brad Hyman, Chana Rothman, Tracey Hill, Rabbi Lauren Tuchman, Jay Stanton, Dr. Ora Horn Prouser, Rabbi Jeff Hoffman, Rabbi Jill Hammer, Rabbi James Stone Goodman, Rabbi Lizz Goldstein, Arielle Cohen, Rabbi Emma Gottlieb, Rabbi Elisa Koppel, Kohenet Annie Matan, Steven Goldstein, Bella Book, Shani Leead, Rabbi Drew Kaplan, Zabeen Khamisa, Dr. Laura Mae Lindo, Dr. Idrisa Pandit, Dr. Doris Jakobsh, Kelly Steiss, Hila Ratzabi, Stacey Zisook Robinson, Trisha Arlin, Rabbi Rachel Barenblat, Debra Nussbaum Cohen, Shelley Schweitzer, Carly Boyce, Ali Bloch, Stephanie Sanger-Miller, Katie Cowie-Redekopp, Mary Lou Klassen, j wallace skelton, Samantha Estoesta Williams, Dr. Elana Maryles Sztokman, Mātā Amṛtānandamayī Devī, Kandace Boos, whose art reveals us all, and my love, Joshua Lieblein, who teaches and manifests wisdom of the heart better than any person I know.

ABOUT THE AUTHOR

Devon Spier drew a map to her ancestors and her heart started beating again. She is a writer and rabbinical student at the Academy for Jewish Religion in New York.

Heart Map and the Song of Our Ancestors is her first book.

ABOUT THE ILLUSTRATOR

Kandace practices mixed-media visual art, often blending the sacred with the everyday, in her home studio in KW. She works at Mennonite Central Committee Ontario with the Indigenous Neighbours program, and is raising two children under 5 with her partner of 6 years.